DID YOU KNOW?
SPORTS

I0799018

20 THINGS YOU DIDN'T KNOW ABOUT

BASKETBALL

THEIA LAKE

PowerKiDS press

Published in 2026 by The Rosen Publishing Group, Inc.
2544 Clinton Street, Buffalo, NY 14224

Portions of this work were originally authored by Ryan Nagelhout and published as *20 Fun Facts About Basketball*. All new material in this edition was authored by Theia Lake.

Some of the images in this book illustrate individuals who are models. The depictions do not imply actual situations or events.

Editor: Greg Roza
Book Design: Tanya Dellaccio Keeney

Photo Credits: Cover Monkey Business Images/Shutterstock.com; p. 5 Historic Collection/Alamy Images; p. 6 Hum Images/Alamy Images; p. 7 hutch photography/Shutterstock.com; p. 8 https://upload.wikimedia.org/wikipedia/commons/2/28/1922_Spalding_basketball.jpg; p. 9 Vitalii Vitleo/Shutterstock.com; p. 10 Courtesy of the Seattle Municiple Archives/Flickr.com; p. 12 Alon Alexander/Alamy Images; p. 13 Cal Sport Media/Alamy Images; p. 14 UPI/Alamy Images; p. 15 (logo) CryptoFX/Shutterstock.com; p. 15 (Jerry West) https://upload.wikimedia.org/wikipedia/commons/5/5a/Jerry_West_1972.jpeg; p. 16 https://upload.wikimedia.org/wikipedia/commons/4/4b/New_York_Knicks_vs._Detroit_Pistons_December_2021_24_%28free_throw%29.jpg; p. 17 Anucha Tiemsom/Shutterstock.com; p. 18 RLFE Pix/Alamy Images; p. 19 Underwood Archives, Inc/Alamy Images; p. 20 Jonathan Kirn/Alamy Images; p. 21 dpa picture alliance/Alamy Images; p. 22 UPI/Alamy Images; p. 23 zhangjin_net/Shutterstock.com; p. 24 ZUMA Press, Inc./Alamy Images; p. 25 https://upload.wikimedia.org/wikipedia/commons/4/4a/Walter_A_Brown_Trophy.png; p. 26 Keeton Gale/Shutterstock.com; p. 27 https://upload.wikimedia.org/wikipedia/commons/5/56/Caitlin_Clark_Final_Four_2024.jpg; p. 29 https://upload.wikimedia.org/wikipedia/commons/7/7a/Cynthia_Cooper_44.jpg.

Cataloging-in-Publication Data
Names: Lake, Theia, author.
Title: 20 things you didn't know about basketball / Theia Lake.
Other titles: Twenty things you didn't know about basketball
Description: Buffalo : PowerKids Press, [2026] | Series: Did you know? sports | Includes index.
Identifiers: LCCN 2025000224 (print) | LCCN 2025000225 (ebook) | ISBN 9781499450330 (library binding) | ISBN 9781499450323 (paperback) | ISBN 9781499450347 (ebook)
Subjects: LCSH: Basketball–Miscellanea–Juvenile literature.
Classification: LCC GV885.1 .L35 2026 (print) | LCC GV885.1 (ebook) | DDC 796.323–dc23/eng/20250106
LC record available at https://lccn.loc.gov/2025000224
LC ebook record available at https://lccn.loc.gov/2025000225

Manufactured in the United States of America

CPSIA Compliance Information: Batch #CSPK26. For Further Information contact Rosen Publishing at 1-800-237-9932.

CONTENTS

THE START OF SOMETHING GREAT

In the winter of 1891–1892, Dr. James Naismith, a teacher at the YMCA in Springfield, Massachusetts, invented an indoor game that could be played between football and baseball seasons. Called "basket ball," his students took to it right away.

Basketball has become much more than a winter sport for students. The National Basketball **Association** (NBA) is the top men's league in the world, with teams in the United States and Canada. The Women's National Basketball Association (WNBA) is the top women's basketball league.

Canadian-born Naismith remained an important figure in basketball his entire life. He was the first basketball coach at the University of Kansas from 1898 to 1907. He was the athletic director of the U of K from 1919 until 1937.

BASKETS AND HOOPS

DID YOU KNOW?

Naismith wrote the original 13 rules for the game he called "basket ball."

Naismith first chose a soccer ball for his new game. Nine players were on each team until 1897, when it was changed to five. Dribbling the ball (bouncing when moving with the ball) wasn't a part of the rules at that time. Hitting the ball with your fist was a **foul**!

Naismith settled on nine players for each team because he usually had 18 students in his class.

The peach baskets were hung 10 feet (3 m) off the ground. Today, basketball hoops in the pros are also 10 feet off the ground.

DID YOU KNOW?

The first basketball "hoops" were baskets used to carry peaches.

In early basketball games, when a basket was scored, the game was stopped and a ladder was brought out to get the ball out of the peach basket. A hole was later cut into the bottom of the baskets so they didn't have to stop the game.

GIMMIE THE BALL

DID YOU KNOW?

The NBA has always used leather basketballs...except for 2 months.

In 2006, the league changed to synthetic (man-made) balls that didn't need to be broken in. The balls stuck to players' hands and often stuck between the rim and backboard. These balls were used for only 2 months before the NBA switched back to leather basketballs.

After using soccer balls for the first two years, the first basketballs were made. They had laces much like footballs do.

DID YOU KNOW?

NBA players get to test and choose three "game balls" before every game.

The first lace-less basketballs were used in 1948. The size had been reduced to a diameter of 30 inches (76 cm).

One player from each team gets to try out leather basketballs and pick their favorites. The three balls both teams like are used in the game. Some players even smell basketballs to pick their game balls!

BASKETBALL LEAGUES

DID YOU KNOW?

The NBA wasn't the first professional basketball league in the Unites States.

In 1949, the NBA formed when the Basketball Association of America (BAA) and the National Basketball League (NBL) **merged** after competing for 3 years. In 1976, four teams from the American Basketball Association (ABA) joined the NBA when that league ended.

The Seattle Supersonics and the Portland Trail Blazers face each other in 1967.

THE NBA/ABA MERGER

NBA TEAMS

Seattle
Portland
Golden State
Los Angeles
Phoenix
Kansas City
Houston
New Orleans
Milwaukee
Chicago
Detroit
Cleveland
Atlanta
Buffalo
Philadelphia
Washington
Boston

ABA TEAMS THAT JOIN NBA

Denver
Indianapolis
San Antonio

CITY WITH BOTH NBA AND ABA TEAM

New York

ABA TEAMS BOUGHT OUT

St Louis
Kentucky

FOLDED BEFORE MERGER

Virginia

DID YOU KNOW?

For the 1948–1950 season, the NBA had 17 teams, some in smaller cities. The NBA once had a team that played for 3 cities.

The Tri-Cities Blackhawks played for three cities: Moline, Illinois; Rock Island, Illinois; and Davenport, Iowa. The state of Indiana had three teams—the Fort Wayne Pistons, Anderson Packers, and Indianapolis Olympians. Other small cities with teams included Waterloo, Iowa, and Sheboygan, Wisconsin.

The Boston Celtics and the Fort Wayne Pistons fight for the ball during a game in 1957.

The Clippers moved to San Diego in 1978 from Buffalo, New York, where the team was first called the Braves.

DID YOU KNOW?

Both Los Angeles teams have kept the nicknames from the cities their **franchise** used to play in.

The LA Lakers moved from Minneapolis, Minnesota, in 1960. The "Lakers" name is a reference to the many lakes in the state of Minnesota. The LA Clippers were moved from the coastal city of San Diego in 1984. A "clipper" is a fast sailboat.

DID YOU KNOW?

The Buffalo Braves and Boston Celtics once traded entire teams.

In 1978, Celtics owner Irving H. Levin and Braves owner John Y. Brown swapped franchises! Levin wanted to move a team west and thought moving the Braves—an **expansion team** just 8 years old—would be easier.

The franchise swap was even weirder because the teams made a 6-player trade after they traded owners!

JERRY WEST

The NBA won't actually say it's West on "The Logo" because they might have to pay him to use his image!

DID YOU KNOW?

The NBA logo is based on a real player.

The figure of Lakers **legend** Jerry West became the NBA logo in 1969. Artist Alan Siegel found a photo of West dribbling down the court and modeled his logo after it. In 2010, Siegel told a newspaper that the logo was in fact West.

THREE POINTS!

DID YOU KNOW?

The NBA first added the 3-point shot in 1979.

The ABL added the 3-point shot in 1961. Since then, the 3-point line has moved back several times and now sits 22 feet (6.7 m) from the hoop in the corners and 23 feet 9 inches (7.2 m) on the **arc**.

An early 3-point line sat just 19 feet (5.8 m) from the basket.

LINES ON THE COURT

Here are the different court lines in the men's and women's pro and college games.

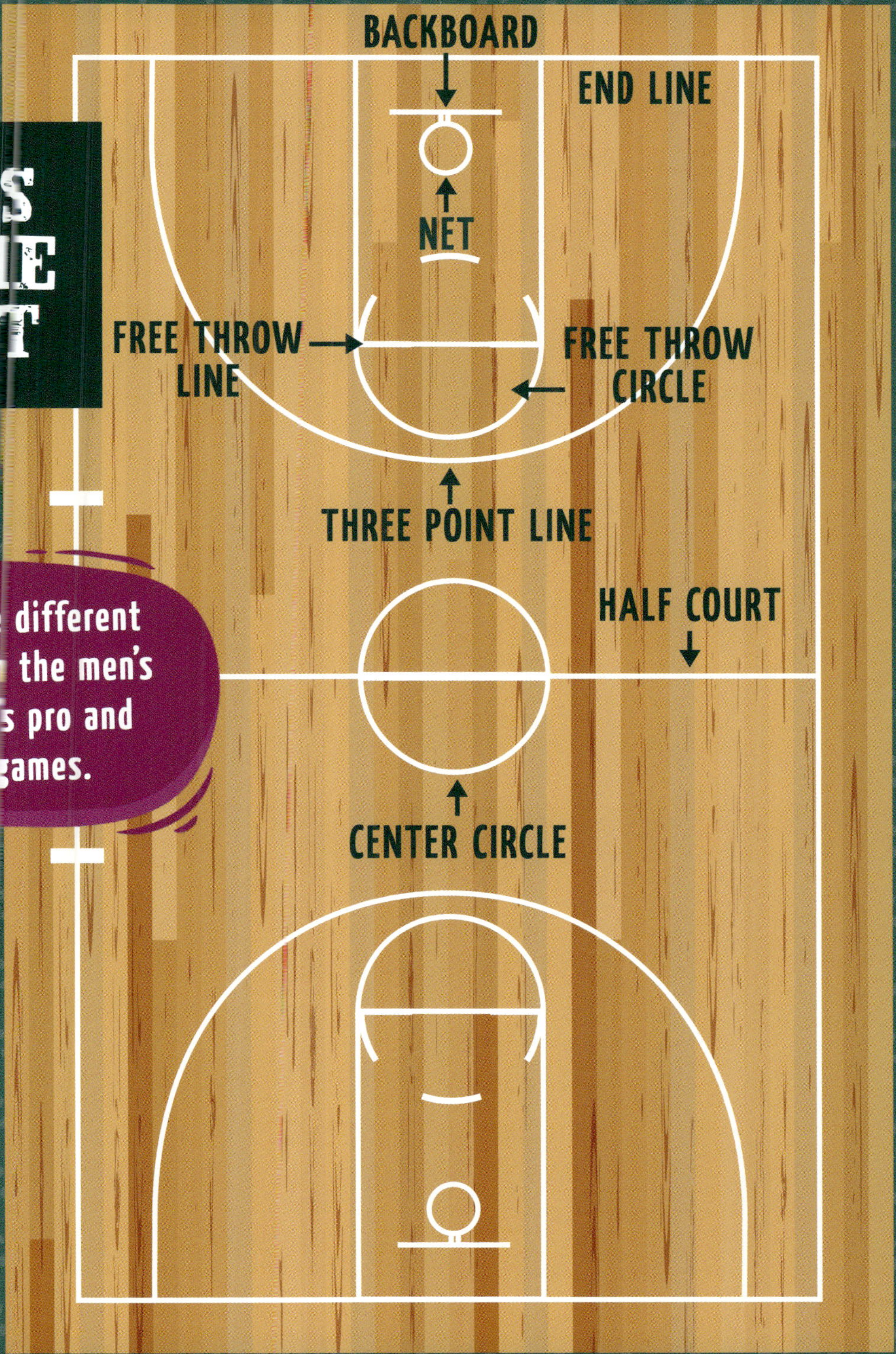

"WILT THE STILT"

DID YOU KNOW?

Wilt Chamberlain once scored 100 points in a game—by himself!

While playing for the Philadelphia Warriors in 1962, Wilt Chamberlain scored exactly 100 points. Chamberlain made 36 shots from the field and hit 28 free throws in a 169–147 win over the New York Knicks on March 2.

Chamberlain earned the nickname "Wilt the Stilt" because of his height—7 foot, 1 inch (216 cm).

Chamberlain still holds the record for most regular-season rebounds during a career with 23,924!

DID YOU KNOW?

Chamberlain played for 14 years and never fouled out of a game!

Chamberlain played 1,045 regular season and 160 playoff games in his career without fouling out. That's 55,418 total minutes without ever picking up a sixth, and final, foul!

PLAYERS ON THE COURT

DID YOU KNOW?

The shortest and tallest players in NBA history were on the same team.

During the 1987–1988 season, Manute Bol played on the Washington Bullets with Muggsy Bogues. Bol was a 7-foot-7-inch (231 cm) center and the tallest player in NBA history (tied with Gheorge Muresan). Bogues was the shortest player in the league at 5 feet 3 inches (160 cm).

Bol's the only player in history to have more blocks (2,086) than points scored (1,599)!

Duncan couldn't practice swimming in the ocean because he was scared of sharks!

DID YOU KNOW?

NBA great Tim Duncan turned to basketball because of hurricanes and sharks!

Duncan grew up in St. Croix, U.S. Virgin Islands. He was a great swimmer and was training for the Olympics until a storm destroyed the only Olympic-sized pool on the island. He turned to basketball and became a two-time NBA Most **Valuable** Player (MVP)!

STRANGE NUMBERS

DID YOU KNOW?

In 1950, the Fort Wayne Pistons beat the Minneapolis Lakers, 19–18!

The lowest-scoring game in NBA history saw the Pistons outscore the Lakers 3–1 in the fourth quarter. The lowest-scoring game in the shot-clock era was between the Celtics and Hawks. The Celtics won, 62–57, in 1955.

In 2015, the New York Knicks and Orlando Magic played the lowest-scoring quarter. The Knicks outscored the Magic, 8–7!

The shot clock was added to stop teams from standing with the ball and not trying to score. Some teams held on to the ball for minutes on end!

DID YOU KNOW?

The 24-second shot clock came from a math problem.

The shot clock was added in 1954 by Syracuse Nationals owner Danny Biasone. He noticed teams in high-scoring games took about 60 shots a game. He divided the length of a game—48 minutes (2,880 seconds)—by 120 shots and got 24 seconds for each shot.

DID YOU KNOW?

The Oklahoma Thunder once lost by 73 points!

On December 2, 2021, Memphis Grizzlies beat the Oklahoma Thunder 152–79. During the game, nine of the 12 players on the Grizzlies scored 10 or more points. One of the Grizzlies' best players, Ja Morant, didn't even play that day!

Jaren Jackson Jr. was the highest scorer with 27 points.

THE TROPHY

The original NBA Championship Finals trophy was named after former Celtics owner Walter A. Brown. In 1984, a new trophy was made. Named after NBA **commissioner** Larry O'Brien, the trophy has been given to the league champion every year since.

DID YOU KNOW?

The NBA has awarded a championship **trophy** to the best team since 1949—however, the trophy design changed in 1984.

Winning teams only "owned" the Walter A. Brown Trophy until the next team won a championship. The winning team gets to keep the Larry O'Brien Trophy—a new one is made each year.

GREATS OF THE WNBA

DID YOU KNOW?

Diana Taurasi won five WNBA scoring titles, including four in a row.

Taurasi was the first overall pick in the 2004 WNBA **draft**. She won her first scoring title with the Phoenix Mercury in 2006. Taurasi then won the league scoring crown from 2008 to 2011! She won the league's Most Valuable Player award during the 2008–2009 season.

Taurasi helped the Mercury win the WNBA title in 2007, 2009, and 2014.

DID YOU KNOW?

Caitlin Clark, a record-breaking college player, continued to break records as a rookie (first-year player) in the WNBA.

In 2024, many fans expected Caitlin Clark to be an instant help for the team that drafted her—the Indiana Fever. She was! Here are just a few of the WNBA records she set or broke in her rookie year:

- 2024 WNBA Rookie of the Year
- Most points by a rookie (769)
- Single-season record for assists (337)
- First **triple-double** by a rookie
- First triple-double in Fever history

Clearly, Clark had an amazing rookie season. However, she also set the record for most turnovers in a single season (223).

SO MUCH MORE TO LEARN!

The histories of the NBA and WNBA are filled with more cool facts. Teams have moved all over the country over the years. Did you know the Denver Nuggets were once called the Larks and Rockets at different times?

Some teams disappeared, only to have new ones take their place. Many players—Chucky Brown and Jim Jackson to name a few—have suited up for a dozen NBA teams in their careers. Did you know Drew Gooden played for 10 different teams in 12 seasons? As each season passes, the league creates more hoops history. Think of all the basketball facts left to discover!

In 1997, at age 34, Cynthia Cooper-Dyke joined the WNBA team the Houston Comets. She led the Comets to 4 championships in 4 straight years. She was the first woman voted into the Naismith Basketball Hall of Fame in 2010.

GLOSSARY

arc: Part of a curved line.

association: A group with common interests.

commissioner: The person in charge of a league.

draft: To pick players for a team.

expansion team: A team newly added to the league.

foul: In basketball, to break a rule.

franchise: A team that's part of a certain league.

legend: In sports, a player well known for their skills and success.

merge: To come together as one.

triple-double: Scoring in the double digits (10 or more) in 3 of 5 categories in one game: points, assists, rebounds, blocks, and steals.

trophy: A prize given for winning.

valuable: Having a lot of skill that helps a team.

FOR MORE INFORMATION

BOOKS

Leed, Percy. *Basketball's NBA and WNBA Finals.* Minneapolis, MN: Lerner Publications, 2025.

Simon, Bradley. *The Most Amazing Basketball Stories of All Time for Kids.* Independently Published, 2023.

WEBSITES

Original 13 Rules of Basketball

www.usab.com/dr-james-naismiths-original-13-rules-of-basketball

Read the original 13 rules of basketball here.

National Basketball Association

nba.com

Find out more about players and teams in the NBA.

Women's National Basketball Association

www.wnba.com

Read all about the WNBA and it's players here.

Publisher's note to educators and parents: Our editors have carefully reviewed these websites to ensure that they are suitable for students. Many websites change frequently, however, and we cannot guarantee that a site's future contents will continue to meet our high standards of quality and educational value. Be advised that students should be closely supervised whenever they access the internet.

INDEX